Cooper's Challenge

Author and Photographer

Susan Brown-Wadleigh

Copyright © 2022 Susan Brown-Wadleigh

All rights reserved.

ISBN: 9798218045630

All rights reserved. No part of this publication may be reproduced or transmitted in any form, or by any means electronic or mechanical including, photocopying, recording, or by any retrieval system without prior written permission from the author.

TABLE OF CONTENTS

1 Cooper   Pg 1

2 Adversity Strikes   Pg 12

3 Cooper Finds the Courage   Pg 16

4 Cooper Carries On   Pg 20

DEDICATION

To Cooper who has shown courage and patience in the face of adversity.

To the Veterinarians and the Veterinarian Specialist who have helped Cooper throughout his journey.

Finally, to my father, who faced physical challenges during his very long and adventurous life. With each new obstacle, he found ways to adapt so that he could continue doing the things he loved: learning and creating.

CHAPTER ONE
COOPER

He loved to play ball.

He jumped jumps.

He tunneled through tunnels.

He found treasures hidden in boxes.

He posed for pictures,

He tamed the wildest of beasts.

CHAPTER TWO
ADVERSITY STRIKES

Then one day, Cooper got sick.

Soon he went blind.

He was frightened, and confused.

CHAPTER THREE
COOPER FINDS THE COURAGE

His friends said, "We love you Cooper."

"Come play with us!"

And...

he did!

CHAPTER FOUR
COOPER CARRIES ON

He still loves to play ball. It takes him a little longer to find it, but he never gives up!

He still loves to nap,

and nap...

He still loves to sniff out hidden treasures,

pose for pictures

(well, maybe he doesn't always

"love" to pose),

and he still loves to tame the wildest of beasts.

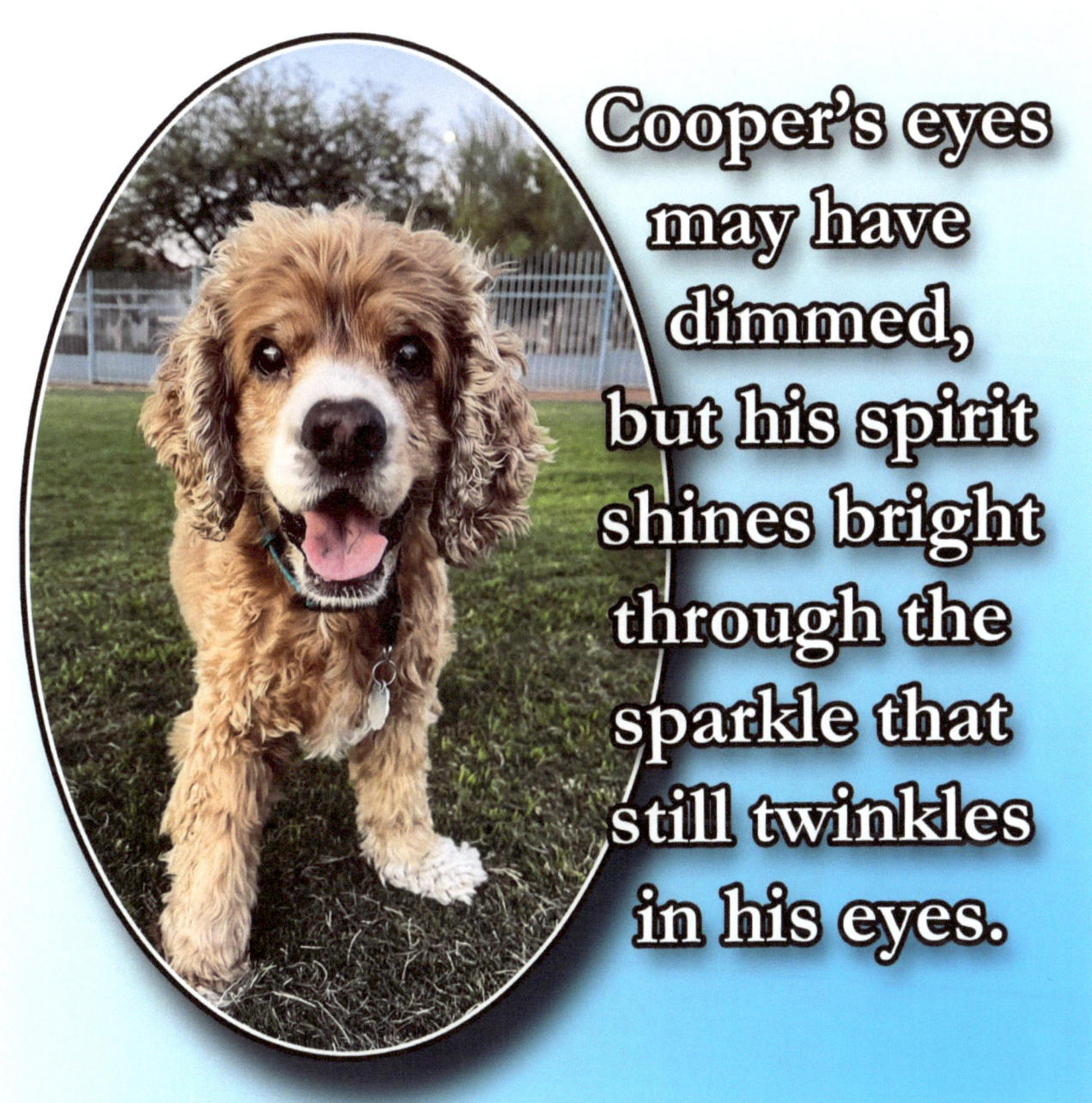

Cooper's eyes may have dimmed, but his spirit shines bright through the sparkle that still twinkles in his eyes.

 Cooper was born on May 23, 2012, he was one of four darling puppies. We picked him for our own because of his white paws and freckled nose.

He was a funny, cute, very smart puppy with a huge attitude. He hated leashes. He loved to learn new things. We had many fun adventures. Cooper was thrilled when we went to the dog park. He particularly enjoyed playing with the big dogs. Fetching the ball was the best! We took agility classes. He liked them but he was easily distracted. On occasion, Cooper would veer off the course, grab one of the little orange cones sitting at the side, and run joyfully across the field holding the prize high over his head, shaking it with glee. We took a Good Citizen course, but he found it very boring. Then we tried a scent class. He trained to sniff out certain odors. Cooper loved the class and was very good at finding those smells anywhere.

In 2017 Cooper was diagnosed with diabetes. A year later he began to lose his eyesight due to cataracts that grew because of his illness.

He is now ten years old. He gets two shots a day of insulin and many eye drops. He endures these procedures patiently with only an annoyed growl now and then. Cooper still loves to play ball. He tells me when it is stuck under a piece of furniture and won't move away from the spot until I retrieve it. He enjoys the dog park and loves it when the other dogs want to play with him. He plays ball there too. It takes him a long time to find the ball in the big field, but he never gives up.

He has been and will always be my inspiration.

www.ingramcontent.com/pod-product-compliance
Lightning Source LLC
Chambersburg PA
CBHW041536040426
42446CB00002B/109